Book 5

TELL
YOUR CHILDREN
ABOUT US

The Dutch in Wartime
Survivors Remember

Edited by

Anne van Arragon Hutten

Mokeham Publishing Inc.

© 2012 Mokeham Publishing Inc.
Box 20203, Penticton, B.C., V2A 8M1, Canada
PO Box 2090, Oroville, WA, 98844, USA
www.mokeham.com

Cover photograph by Sanne Terpstra

ISBN 978-0-9868308-6-0

Contents

On the front cover

The 'Contemplation Monument' in North-Amsterdam was erected to remind the citizens of Amsterdam of the casualties of war and regained freedom and peace. Behind a seated pensive woman are four granite slabs. Three of these show images of people with their hands above their head. The fourth has a quote from a farewell letter written by Resistance fighter Krijn Breurs, before his execution in February of 1943:

Tell your children about us and our struggle and the life that we desire. May our greatest longings be surpassed by life itself. Work and love, fight and win. Live! Live all and grow tall.

The monument was created by Marius van Beek and unveiled on May 4, 1983.

Introduction

Anne van Arragon Hutten

A year or two before my Aunt Gerda died, she told me the story of her wedding dress.

All my life I had heard stories and read books about the war and about the shortages of everything we normally consider essential, but her story drove it home for me.

The year was 1945, and she was getting married at last. Like all brides, she started thinking about a wedding gown. And like most rural brides in the province of Overijssel of that time, it would be a black dress, with perhaps a bit of lace trim at the neck. But where to get such a gown? The stores were empty, and fabric could not be bought at any price.

Gerda knew who to ask. One of her older sisters, Mina, had two seamstress diplomas and could sew anything. And as Gerda had hoped, Mina came up with a solution. She managed to get her hands on two old men's overcoats, which in those days had a silk lining. She removed the lining with great care, carefully took apart every seam, washed and ironed it. Then she laid pattern pieces on the fabric and began cutting. The end result was an elegant gown that Gerda was proud to wear.

Mina, as it turned out, became my mother some years later, and that gives this story extra meaning for me. But mostly Gerda's wedding gown represents the ingenuity, the creativity, and the sheer stubborn resilience displayed by the Dutch in general, when they refused to lie down and cry in the face of so much deprivation. As you will read in this book, the population of Holland used their wits in dealing with an oppressor who stole all that was rightfully theirs, leaving the rightful owners without sufficient food, clothing, and footwear.

The Germans requisitioned (read: stole) whatever they wanted. They needed ships for their ultimately unsuccessful quest to conquer England, and Holland's fishermen were required to give them up even though that meant a complete loss of their livelihood. They needed copper, and not only was every household required to bring copper items to the town hall, but even church bells were taken down to be melted down for the war effort. They needed bicycles for their troops, and each family had to hand one over. Germany had drafted so many of its men to fight their war that hardly anyone remained to work the factories that made the weapons, and so even men and boys were requisitioned, or rather, forcibly taken.

How does a small country like Holland continue to function without the necessities of life? Obviously, it did so with great difficulty. And yet people carried on, trying for some semblance of normality. Children still went to school, until school buildings were requisitioned too, or a lack of fuel made it impossible. With one-third of a million men in hiding, many women and boys took over the responsibility of obtaining food and fuel, the most basic requirements everywhere. Children as young as six served as couriers for underground newsletters. Families continued to celebrate birthdays, Saint Nicholas, and Christmas, however meager the food.

They somehow absorbed the continually increasing

loss of freedom, loss of property rights, and even the loss of family members to slave labour, captivity, or death. It's the British who are famous for keeping a stiff upper lip, but it seems to me that the wartime Dutch may have demonstrated this quality in equal measure. The Dutch never lost their hope that eventually Hitler's reign would end, that liberation would some day come. In the meantime they simply endured all the hardships, not knowing that the worst was yet to come.

This volume of The Dutch In Wartime mostly deals with the personal stories of families and individuals who carried on despite aerial battles overhead, V-1 and V-2 rockets crashing prematurely, hostile German soldiers on every street corner and sometimes at the door in the middle of the night. The ultimate battle to liberate the country, and the Hunger Winter that preceded it, still lay mostly in the future.

Historical Background

Tom Bijvoet

As the occupation lasted longer, and ever more resources were being drawn out of the occupied territories to fuel the German war machine, the outlook for Holland's civilian population became increasingly bleak. Rations were getting smaller. And what little there was, was often of inferior quality. Clothing, shoes, furniture, everything had to be made to last and many items were falling into disrepair and had to be continually patched up. Commodities and services that even in the impoverished pre-war depression years had been taken for granted, were becoming luxury items: soap, fuel, and transportation among them.

And there was no end in sight. The long anticipated second military front that had been hoped for first in 1942 and then expected in 1943 did not seem to want to materialize. By the spring of 1944 the occupation had lasted for four full years. Four full years of repression, scarcity, the struggle to put a meal on the table, to clothe one's family, and heat one's home. A struggle that often did not deliver adequate results.

Although most people's lives were not in immediate danger, there was always the risk of becoming an unintended victim of 'friendly fire'. Allied bombs intended for military or industrial targets would occasionally miss and fall on city neighborhoods, as happened among other places in Rotterdam on March 31, 1943 (400 dead), Amsterdam on July 17, 1943 (150 dead) and Nijmegen on February 22, 1944 (800 dead). An

Allied plane on its way home from a raid on Germany could be hit by flak and crash into a farm, village or town and Allied aircraft could strafe trains and ships carrying civilians that were mistaken for, or combined with, military transports.

Starting in mid-June, 1944, hundreds of V-1 and later V-2 missiles were launched from Dutch soil, aimed at targets in England and Belgium. When a launch failed, as happened on occasion, these flying bombs often dropped on nearby neighbourhoods. And then there was the ever present danger of being rounded up by the Germans in an act of retribution against Resistance activity or being sent to Germany to work in factories that were bombed almost daily by the Allied air forces.

When finally on June 6, 1944 the Allied landings in Normandy took place there seemed to be light at the end of the tunnel. The Allies progressed rapidly. They liberated Paris on August 25, Brussels on September 3, and Antwerp on September 4. By Tuesday, September 5, it seemed as though the liberation of western Europe was all but over. Rumours, some misinformation in an English radio broadcast, and four years of pent-up hope led to the widespread belief that the Allies had already reached Holland and that the country would be free within a matter of days. Chaotic scenes ensued on this day, which has become known as 'Crazy Tuesday'. Germans and collaborators fled east, people who had been in hiding surfaced and streets were lined with flag-waving citizens awaiting the first Allied troops.

But the speed of the advance had caught up with the Allies, who had run into significant logistical problems. The troops that had reached Antwerp were advance units only. It was impossible for the vast mass of the

Allied armies needed to liberate the rest of Europe to move that fast. Despite that, on September 12 the Allies crossed the Dutch border south of Maastricht, which, two days later, was the first major Dutch city to be liberated. Other sections of Limburg, Brabant, and Zeeland were also liberated in the fall of 1944. But the Allied advance into The Netherlands came to an abrupt halt when Operation Market Garden, the airborne operation intended to push across the Rhine at Arnhem, ended in failure. The battle, which started on September 17, eventually gave rise to many books and movies, such as *A Bridge Too Far*. It is the subject of the seventh volume in this series.

After 'Crazy Tuesday', German forces brutally re-established control over their own fleeing troops and the Dutch population. This was the start of the most oppressive, brutal, harsh, and devastating period of the occupation, known as the Hunger Winter, which is covered in the eighth volume of the series.

Remembrance of a War

Gerry Bijwaard

World War II started for me on May 10, 1940. I was eight years old. For many months I had heard my parents talk about the possibility of Nazi troops invading my small, native country, but it had made very little impact on my thinking. After all, our government had declared itself neutral, and no nation would do such a treacherous thing as invade a little, peace-loving country that wanted to be left alone. I can, of course, be excused for my naiveté because of my age, but the invasion of my country on that fateful day in May left a mark on me for the rest of my life. The day I saw German tanks come down the street where my family lived, is still fresh in my memory. I can still see the grim faces of our neighbors and friends who, together with my parents, knew the meaning of being occupied by foreign troops: losing the freedom we had enjoyed so much since the end of the Napoleonic era, seeing our country destroyed and plundered, and losing many of its citizens to violence, hunger, and disease. It took five long years before I saw the first Canadian tank come down that same street – a happy sight indeed.

In the years that followed the German invasion, our way of life increasingly deteriorated. Food and clothing became scarce; young men between the ages of 18 and 40 were rounded up and transported to Germany to work in Hitler's factories; medical care became nonexistent; Jews disappeared; and violence was all around us.

11

Holland's people suffered, especially in the cold winter of 1944-45, which became known as the Hunger Winter, in which many thousands of people starved to death or became victims of disease, especially diphtheria.

Like all kids I was fascinated by airplanes and other machines of war. I learned to recognize the difference between American, British, and German planes even when they were at great heights. I knew all their names and their capabilities. At night I would lie in bed listening to the constant drone of the many planes, always wondering what it would be like to fly in one of them. When they started to come over during daylight hours on their way to Germany, my neighborhood friends and I would count them, lying in the meadow facing the sky. It would often go on for hours. One time we counted close to 350 planes. We did not have the faintest idea where exactly they were going and what destruction they were capable of, but my father, who often listened to the BBC broadcast in German on our clandestine radio, would mention Schweinfurt, Regensburg, Hamburg, Berlin, or the Ruhr. One time in February, he mentioned Dresden. It was only much later that we learned what had taken place there, but that news came from other sources, because the Allies kept the results secret for reasons now well known.

Towards the beginning of the terrible winter of 1944-45, the Allied raids became more frequent. The flying armadas were accompanied by fighter planes, which kept the German fighters at a safe distance. There was no anti-aircraft close to my hometown, but we could hear it in the far distance and would wonder what it was like to fly through the flak of exploding projectiles. "It must have been the flak," we said, that crippled the B17 we saw during the last war winter. It met its end close to the little village of Zegveld, about 50 miles south of Amsterdam, and remains the final resting place of several members of an American bomber crew. It happened in the final phase of WW II, when the plane struggled to return to its base in England after a bombing raid over Germany. The plane, flying on only one of its four engines, was no match for the Messerschmitts who brutally and effectively finished it off. We watched closely when we heard the B-17's last remaining propeller chop the cold air. It was a strangely different sound and because the plane was so low, we saw it as a giant silhouette against the gray sky. Its 32-meter-wide wingspan seemed enormous, and I could see the gunner in the tail. I could also see flames flaring from one of its sides. Seven Messerschmitts encircled it, relentlessly firing their deadly weapons until the B17 lost more height and finally dove into the soggy, heavy clay of Holland's low country, where it will remain forever. This was followed by two white parachutes of crewmembers who were lucky enough to bail out. Many years later I learned their names: Barclay W. Glover from Philadelphia and Charles D. Barnthson from somewhere in Kansas. One body that was recovered at the time was that of George L. Armberg. I recorded the date and the hour in my little notebook: February 21, 1945, 14:40 hr, although I never needed the notebook to recall the date or the hour.

Shortly after the war, an attempt was made to lift the plane, but the salvage equipment was too heavy for the soggy terrain, and the project was abandoned. The plane had slowly sunk into the wet soil to disappear forever from sight. Cows now graze nearby. Someone put a steel pipe in the ground to mark the location. Methane gas bubbles coming out of this pipe serve as a reminder that the wreck may not have come to rest yet. Some years ago I learned that both Glover and Barnthson had been taken prisoner, together with some people from the village who had tried to help them with their wounds. All were fortunate and were released after the war.

There was no upstairs left

Els Bauman

The German soldiers confiscated most of the food that was produced, and sent it to Germany for people there. Food, therefore, became extremely scarce. The farm my father worked on no longer grew anything, as the farmer didn't want to feed the enemy. As a result my father lost his job. Soon he got another job, working for the Civil Air Defense. He was stationed on top of the highest church tower in Deventer, where he had to report British or German planes coming in. This was necessary so that the sirens could be started to quickly warn the people to take shelter. Life went on and people adjusted, but many became homeless.

In 1944, Germany started testing its long-range rockets. They were aiming them at England but many crashed in Holland. Whenever a rocket was coming our way, sirens went off and we would go into our cellars until we heard the 'all clear' signal. During this time, my brother, Gerard, was born, on January 9, 1944. One day that summer the sirens went off again and Mother, carrying baby Gerard, and my sister Anneke and I went down the cellar steps. I tripped over my wooden shoes and scraped my knees pretty badly but at least we were safe in the cellar.

After we heard the 'all clear' sirens we went back upstairs. To our surprise there was no upstairs left! The rocket had misfired and had crashed not far from where we lived. Many of the homes in our neighbourhood were damaged, while ours was no longer livable. My grandparents lived across the river, so we stayed with them at first. Food was scarce and they didn't have enough for themselves and our family of five.

It was decided that we would go north to Friesland, where my Dad's sister Anna lived. She was married to a farmer. My parents planned to take us kids there by train at night. All that was available were freight trains with windowless boxcars. (I recently heard that Dad had traveled in women's clothes, maybe so the Germans wouldn't pick him up). We managed to get into a boxcar and sat in the dark on the floor. It would go for a while and then stop. By late evening it stopped again and we heard that it would go no farther.

My parents had no idea where we were, so mother asked around and was given the name of a little town. She remembered she knew some people who had moved there. She told us children to stay put until she and my father came back. After what seemed like an eternity they returned to tell us they had found the people and we could stay with them for the night. We were fed supper at their home and spent the night there. The man of the house told us we could catch a ride in the morning on a barge that was going to Friesland. After breakfast the next morning we found the barge and went on board. That trip took most of the day because barges were pushed by a long barge pole. There was no fuel for any kind of motor. After leaving the barge we walked the rest of the way and were very tired. After a quick supper we kids were shuffled off to bed. Anneke and I got to sleep in a bedstee, a closet-bed, which had double doors and was right in the living room so we could hear everything that was being discussed. I think my parents and Jerry slept in the attic.

We stayed there a long time. My father helped with the farm work and my mother helped Aunt Anna with sewing and mending. My mother could patch or mend anything, which was useful because there was nothing new you could buy. Uncle Tjerk had a large cow barn attached to the house. He milked twenty cows, and had three horses in a separate stall. You had to pass the horses to get to the outhouse. I was scared to death every time I had to use the outhouse. One day I was in the barnyard to feed the chickens when a big rooster attacked me. I was only three and a half and feared for my life. I screamed my head off. Just then some German soldiers walked around the corner of the barn and rescued me They told my uncle to chop off the rooster's head and put him in the soup. My uncle replied, "And who's going to mate with my chickens?"

Little stinkers

Tony Stroeve

Tony Stroeve, who escaped to England with ten others in 1943, compares wartime cigarettes to those given them by the British.

While we were in the wardroom on the ship after having finished a good feed, some of us rolled ourselves a cigarette and lit up. It was not long before we were asked to put out our smokes and were each handed a packet of *Senior Service*. Our hosts said they had never smelled such vile tobacco. No wonder. It was a special mixture available on the black market and made in Belgium, known as 'little stinkers' in Holland, and one of the few freely available, for a price of course. There was a special way they had to be smoked. You had to take only small puffs. If you took big puffs, it firstly hit you like a mule's kick and then the cig just kept burning till it reached your lips and fingers. You did get used to it though, and we only rolled them very, very thin. The packet lasted longer, too, that way.

I pedaled
until my legs ached

Elsa Abma

During the occupation of The Netherlands the electrical supply was cut off for several months. My parents and their neighbours became ingenious in compensating for that loss, especially in finding ways to light their homes. At first there were still candles as a light source. Gouda, known mainly for cheese production, was also known for the beautiful dripless candles produced there. However, manufacture, and transportation of products, had come to a complete standstill and the candle supply dwindled fast.

Natural gas was available for a while, and my father constructed a gas line from the gas stove in the kitchen to the lamp over our dining room table. In the evening we sat around that table, reading, mending, and attending to school work, to the hissing, reassuring sound of the lamp. Eventually, even gas became scarce. For a while our oppressors let us have gas till eight in the evening; then we were completely cut off.

Vegetable oil was still available in limited supply. My mother prepared small jars of water, with oil and a cotton wick floating on top. it was a poor light fixture, not enough to read by, but enough to find the stairs on our way to bed. We never did run completely out of vegetable oil.

Another invention was to generate our own electricity

by way of the kitchen faucet. A small water wheel, connected to a bicycle transformer was set in motion by the force of the faucet's water spray. The current would light small flashlight bulbs, which were hung in the kitchen and hall. This 'convenience' took a lot of water and was short-lived, because our water supply was shut off during the last three months of the war. Nevertheless people's resourcefulness did not cease.

Our neighbours attached a small transformer to the wheel of an old Singer sewing machine with pedal power. They could pedal and read a book at the same time. This presented them with a double stimulus, for the body and the mind.

My mother owned a wonderful three-speed bike, which we put in our house on its stand so that the back tire was off the floor. The bike had a transformer connected to its back wheel. I would sit on that bike, pedaling till my legs ached, while my father read the newspaper, tobacco smoke curling lazily from his pipe.

We knew of people who constructed carbide lamps. Carbide light was very bright, enough to thread a needle or read by. They spread a strong, unpleasant odor when brought indoors. Better yet was an odorless outside light source: the full moon. On cloudless evenings we would not pull our blinds because the moon became our natural lamp. Reading would be difficult. However, taking turns playing memorized pieces on the piano created a pleasant atmosphere on those moonlit evenings.

It is amazing how inventive the human mind becomes in times of desperate need!

Those were hard times

Petra Poutsma

When I was six I was bored one day, so my mother told me to bike to the Catholic graveyard to look at the grave of a recently departed neighbour whose land had bordered our back garden.

"Take Theo along," she said. Theo was my two-year-old brother, who was put on the baggage carrier. We started off, but not to the graveyard. I turned into a street not far from our place that went through the polder. All you could see there were pastures with ditches and farmhouses. I had always wondered where this road went. It was gorgeous weather, with a blue sky.

What wasn't so gorgeous was the fact that it was also good weather for the Allies to throw bombs. Soon I heard the droning of airplanes, at first far away, then coming closer until they passed right overhead and started tossing bombs on the rail line to Amersfoort, a little farther on. We called these airplanes *jagertjes*, little hunters, because they were not large and could soar up and down very quickly.

Theo began screaming in fright, and I was in tears too because I thought they wanted to bomb us. We jumped off the bike - a little earlier we had passed a farm - and my little brother ran screaming in that direction. I followed, running beside the bike. A couple of farm maids and hired men stood there, laughing at us while we ran up the driveway.

They gave us a glass of milk, and when the bombing raid was over, we went back home on the bicycle. I don't remember what mother said, but I was probably given a stern warning or a spanking.

Another time I had to go to a farmer who lived some distance away, to get milk. I parked the bike against the wall while waiting for the farmer's wife. There were German soldiers quartered there, as they were on many other farms. A bunch of them stood there in the farmyard, and one short, fat guy grabbed my bike and tried to ride it, to great hilarity of his companions. I flattened myself against the wall and was scared to death that the tires would burst. When he finally was done he just threw the bike down.

A nastier memory is that I, six or seven years old, had to distribute secret messages from the Underground to various addresses, sometimes quite far away. Mother was in the Resistance and hid Jews and other people who had been forced into hiding. She always used to distribute those messages herself but said it was becoming too obvious. No one would suspect a child, she said.

The worst was that I had to ride all the way to Hees, a scary swampy area near Soest. I had to go past pastures and tree stumps to a farm that lay at the back of beyond, and where they wouldn't even let me come in. They just opened the door a crack and took the pamphlets from me. Somewhere on that long country road, with a few poor little houses here and there, there was a little dog that always yapped at me and tried to bite my legs, legs that couldn't just hold still because on this bike the pedals always kept turning.

I was always scared to death, especially if I had to go through a German checkpoint. You never knew where these would be set up. I used to hear my mother telling her friends, "Oh that child isn't afraid of the devil himself...". I couldn't figure that, because I felt more like a weasel than a hero. It's hard to understand now how a parent could send a small child on such dangerous missions, as if the course of the war would have been changed one little bit by whether those secret messages were delivered or not. But then, those were hard times.

A fearful time

Olga Chesbrough

I grew up during the war years, and I remember that during the years when my father worked with the Underground, we moved a lot. The Germans would come into the house, go through all the rooms including bathroom, attic, and garage, to see if they could capture my father. The Germans actually searched one house while my father was hiding there!

As a family of three (after my father went into hiding) we had to leave our house and climb across our neighbours' roofs to escape the soldiers. For a child, that was a fearful time to grow up in.

The factory was bombed

Wilhelmus Bongers

A section of the Resistance was known, perhaps informally, as the ration-card-coupon-forgery-department. My dad became involved in the distribution of the forged coupons it produced.

Our house was built in 1666 and had a unique hiding place between the ceiling of the main floor and the floor above it. It was about three feet deep and stretched across the whole area of the house. It was not detectable from inside or outside the house. Access was gained by removing a floorboard in my parents' bedroom.

Some of the local merchants had been given notice that their goods in stock would be confiscated. De Haan's radio store, for instance, and Lakeman's bicycle shop, and Nelis Verbeek's shoe store. Mr. de Haan brought almost all his radios that he had in stock, one at a time, very carefully, to our house to be hidden in that three-foot secret area. Mr. Lakeman's son, Simon, rode the bicycles one at a time by different routes to our house, with the same three-foot space as destination. Neighbour Verbeek came with dozens of boxes of expensive shoes. When I think about all the risks my parents took, it's a wonder we're alive to tell about it.

In 1943, the Germans went on a plundering rampage through the cities of Holland, Hoorn, where we lived, included, removing the bells out of the church steeples. The two small bells of the harbour tower were the first to go, then the one in the Roman Catholic church, and finally the ones from the big church in the church square. The forty-four bells from this steeple constituted our carillon. I was there when they were taken, as I had just walked from Warmoes Street (Warmoesstraat) onto the square. When all the bells were removed they also took the bronze weather vane from the top of the steeple. This was a dangerous job and took a while to get done. I had always thought it to be a rooster of minimal proportions. The hoist rope fell ten meters short so the weather vane was dropped onto the square with a loud noise, damaging it. I was surprised to see that it was a mermaid, not a rooster, and appeared to be as big as an automobile.

In 1944 Hoorn was startled by two bombers that collided in mid-air, with pieces raining down all over. Everywhere in town where I looked we saw parts of the plane. It was terrible event, which is deeply ingrained in my memory.

When my oldest brother, Joep, was laid off from his work as a blacksmith's assistant, he was sent to Kassel in the centre of Germany to work in an airplane ball-bearing factory.

While working there he gradually developed his own way of sabotage. The bearings they manufactured were mainly roller types rather than the ball types. They were made very precisely. By deviating from this high tolerance and making one roller just fractionally larger than the others in that same bearing, it would pass inspection but its life expectancy was very limited, causing the motor or machine to break down at unexpected, maybe fatal, times. An airplane motor with one of these defective bearings could suddenly conk out, causing the plane to crash.

In 1943 the Allies, using naptha and phosporus bombs, bombed the factory. Several workers, including Joep, were burned. He also lost half his nose. He was taken to the hospital where he was treated for burn wounds, and by removing a small section from his hip they managed to construct a new nose. My parents received notification of his condition from the Red Cross, with the urgent request for clothing, mainly underwear and sweaters.

None of these items were available from the stores any longer, so Mom and two sisters started knitting these from used yarn, obtained by unpicking old sweaters from family members. One of the neighbour women owned a spinning wheel. She came over with it and re-spun some of the yarn.

In the hospital, Joep got acquainted with a man from Poland, one from Czechoslovakia, and another Dutchman from Schiedam. The four of them escaped from the hospital, fled into the mountains, and hid inside a barn belonging to a German farmer. One of the farmer's daughters found them in the morning. The farmer luckily was on their side and kept them hidden till the end of the war. They were expected to help with farm chores and repair some of the farm equipment. Joep wrote home when he could.

I was born in 1941

Tina Hofman

These are my war memories:

- Dad boarding up the living room window with plywood because of the blackouts.
- Going home in pitch darkness from a playmate's birthday party.
- Waking up scared stiff in early morning from the drone of many planes flying over on their way to Germany.
- Being taken to grandparents on the back of Dad's bike as my little brother came into the world in May of 1944.
- A meal of "rabbit" (black and white with long tail).
- A teenage boy on our doorstep asking for a sandwich.
- Celebrating liberation too soon, and being chased away from our little square by two SS soldiers in black, with guns on their shoulders.
- May 5, 1945 Liberation - people going crazy, parading around dressed in funny clothing.
- Dad hoisting the "flag" made from the plywood used to board up the window. It still had the dark reddish brown color as we did not have any red, white, or blue paint.
- On the way to school in 1947, heard that the Jewish doctor and his family had made it back.

I was only seven

Michael Vanderboon

Many families in Holland helped by hiding Jewish people in their homes and on their farms, or helped them escape to Switzerland, but many others were afraid to do so. Some people were in a location where it was absolutely too dangerous, next door to a collaborator for example. My Dad helped by doing work for the underground, personal papers and such, but most of the time he was hiding himself.

For many years I have asked myself what moved people to become rescuers? Why did they risk their lives and that of their families? Why did they go through those many months of anxiety and fear that they might be betrayed, that they might be killed? I think the answer was that we considered these people needing help to be just like us; we thought of them as human beings just as we were.

Sometimes we saw the cattle cars go by with people in them, looking back at us with frightened, hollow eyes. I remember seeing a bunch of drunken Nazis, laughing. For some reason they had taken an old Jewish woman who was walking behind me, dragging her by the hair. I don't know why, perhaps they were drunk, but I remember distinctly that I was terrified.

One morning on my way to school I passed by a small Jewish children's home. The Nazis were loading the children, who ranged in age from babies to around seven or eight, on trucks. The children were upset and crying. When they did not move fast enough, the Nazis picked them up by an arm, a leg, their hair, and threw them into the trucks. To watch grown men treat small children that way… I could not believe my eyes. I found myself literally crying with rage. A couple of women who came running up and started to protest were thrown in the truck also. What could I do? I was only seven.

Would a German shoot a saint?

Tine Steen-Dekker

That night in 1944, our family of Father, Mother, baby sister, and I, were sitting in the living room in anticipation of what was to come. The long velvet curtains were tightly shut, on account of Nazis who, on their evening rounds, would bang on the door with their rifle butts and shout at us if any bit of light showed. The whole country had to be dark all night to avoid making it a target for Allied bombers flying over from Britain. The verdunkling, or blackout, was protection for the Dutch and their oppressors alike.

Our heater warmed the room; we still had some wood to stoke it, which Father had 'organized' for the occasion. My sister Noor was sitting on Mother's lap, I was seated nearby for comfort because I had been told that Saint Nicholas and Black Peter might come, and our back door was unlocked. However, a curfew was in place for after dark, and I wondered what would happen to the saint and Black Peter if a German detected them on the street. Would a German shoot a saint?

Mom and Dad began to sing the traditional songs about our wishes for a gift to be put in the shoes set out by the chimney. We sang about the 'stranger knocking on our door', and about 'seeing a steamboat coming from Spain', bringing the holy man. I could see by Mother's smile that something exciting was soon going to happen. Sure enough, after we had exhausted our repertoire of songs a voice called out, "Are there any naughty children inside?" To my relief, Dad answered, "Not here, Saint Nicholas." And there he was, the real saint, entering the room.

He was as tall as my father and he wore a bright red mantle, floor-length and edged with gold braid. He wore white gloves and carried a small jute bag in one hand and his golden staff in the other. A mustache and sideburns covered most of his face and on his white curls he wore a gold miter. I found it a bit odd that Black Peter was absent, because now the saint had to carry the gifts himself.

Saint Nicholas told us about the difficult time he was having because of the German presence and the shortage of toys and food. But he gave me a small parcel wrapped in brown paper. Opening it, I held a small cloth bag closed with two strings. When I rolled the top back I saw a collection of small balls the size of large cherries, in pink, blue, and purple. I wondered what they could be, and Dad asked if he could have one. He popped one into his mouth and now I knew I had a whole bag of candy.

I was startled by my father's loud moan. Looking up I saw him spitting a mud-coloured mass into one of his hands. He quickly went into the kitchen and we heard water splashing. On his return he laid a hand on my head and said, "A kind of marble, I suppose; it is hard to know by candle light." Saint Nicholas added a comment about power being rationed to a few hours per day, and we chuckled about the mistaken 'candy'.

Dad disappeared downstairs. When he came back up he checked our dark curtains to see if they were fully closed, then flipped the light switch. Our room flooded with light, and we were glad to be able to see so much better. I next received a book of fairy tales and a large wooden puzzle covered in cellophane.

Saint Nicholas and my father had begun a conversation about the advance of the Allied forces and the predicament of the Dutch because of food shortages now that the trains had stopped running. I found it unusual and somewhat strange to see Father and the holy man having such an animated conversation, as if they were the best of friends. But then, I thought, Dad had known the saint for a long time.

I listened while admiring my puzzle, and heard the saint ask Dad how he dared use the electric light at this time of day. We were allowed to use it for a few hours, but never in the evenings. I figured that if a family used more than was allowed, we could be in deep trouble. Then Dad shrugged and said, "I stopped the meter from turning."

"How?" asked the saint, and Dad said, "I think I can trust you to keep this secret. I stopped it by sticking a straight pin inside the case so the meter cannot turn."

Saint Nicholas nodded and said how nice it was to have the light on his special evening. I began reading my book and Mom was getting little Nora ready for bed. Father and the saint talked on and laughed heartily at times. It made me glad to have such a happy atmosphere, but I found the camaraderie unusual as the saint had been reserved when I had seen him in my classroom earlier on. I was surprised too by the length of time he was spending with us. Surely he had other children to visit…

Before Saint Nicholas left he reminded Dad to take that pin out. Dad relit the candles and turned off the lights, then took me on his knee and read me the first story in my book. No Allied planes came over that night.

I woke when it was already daylight and the first thing I thought about was the pin in the meter. In my pajamas I went downstairs, located the meter box, and dragged a chair over. Indeed, I saw it: on a slight slant stood a pin, stopping a metal disc from turning. Should I try to take it out? How did the case open?

I felt a hand on my shoulder and Father whispered, "We both remembered." He lifted me down, and I so regret not having seen how the glass case was opened.

We always had enough to eat

John In 't Hout

On December 2, 1944, the Germans blew up two dykes near Arnhem in an effort to keep the Allied forces back by flooding the area known as De Betuwe, low lying land between the rivers Maas and Waal.

My mother, my little brother and I had been evacuated from Scheveningen because we lived too close to where the Atlantikwall was being built. My mother and my brother had been sent to live with a farmer, I had been sent to live with a miller and his wife who had three daughters. We were confronted with the fact that the Germans inundated the Maas and Waal area because the Germans were on one side and the British on the other. In no time at all, the houses were largely under water. Since we lived in a two-storey house the whole family went upstairs. In the town there was a man who made wooden shoes. He had various logs, which drifted away as we watched from the upstairs windows.

Probably because I was still quite young it occurred to me that I could go and look for my mother and brother. I even managed to get hold of a log in an effort to find them.

After the water level had gone down again, we evacuees had to report to the Germans who then took us to Schalkwijk. I have to say I don't know what hunger is.

We always had enough to eat, even as we saw people from Rotterdam walking along, trying to trade their bed sheets for bread. In Schalkwijk we got pea soup to eat, and that soup would be repeated for ten days straight, morning, noon, and night. To this day, my brother won't even look at pea soup.

Some of us who had been evacuated from Scheveningen were then put on a train to Friesland, arriving in Kornwerd close to Makkum. Again I was separated from my mother and brother and was housed with a man who worked at a plant nursery, while my mother and brother went to a carpenter's family. We got there on a Friday, and wouldn't you know it, their custom was to eat pea soup on Fridays.

After Liberation we finally returned to Scheveningen by boat across IJssel Lake, then by a Red Cross vehicle to our home. On arrival, we found that the brick structure had survived, but every bit of wood for doors, floors and whatnot had been removed. The people who had been permitted to remain in the town had taken what they could in order to stay warm that last winter. We had to live with relatives in The Hague for a long time before we could move to a rented house in Scheveningen. Our furniture had been stored elsewhere, so we were able to retrieve that.

She gave me a chicken egg for my birthday

Pauline Hofman

It was 1944 and my tenth birthday was approaching. Not that I had any wishes except for hoping that my fear of airplanes and of the German soldiers everywhere would disappear somehow. I had walked to church that morning with my sister Kea, and after breakfast I skipped to our next-door neighbour's place where my friend Riekie was helping her Dad in the barn. Some time later she decided to check with her Mom to see if I could stay for lunch. The midday meal at their house on Sunday was always such a treat. They had better food than we did; they were farmers. Her mother did invite me to join them, and I ran home to check with my family.

As I rounded the corner of their yard, approaching the alley which connected both our yards, I suddenly heard a familiar screeching sound. An airplane was approaching very low and at high speed, and as I looked for shelter, not really knowing where to go, I ran and crouched behind a stone wall. I heard a whistling sound and then a big bang and something exploding. I felt the ground rolling under me and sensed something falling close by. My mind was racing: is there another plane coming? Where did this bomb fall? How close?

I heard my mother call out, and I made a dash for home, hoping there was not another plane coming and dropping another bomb. It stayed quiet. My heart was

37

pounding as I entered the house, feeling safe to see some of my family. I noticed the windows had blown out. Glass was everywhere. The leaded glass in the doors between the dining room and living room was shattered.

My sisters came home from a late mass they had attended. They had heard the attack while in church. The priest had stopped the service, and as soon as all was quiet the parishioners had gone home. My sisters were pretty shaken, as we all were. My uncle Adriaan and cousin Gerry came to our house. They had heard that a bomb had fallen in our neighbourhood, only a few backyards from ours. The two of them boarded up our house and invited us to come and spend the night with them. Before we left I ran over to tell the neighbours, and in the space where I had crouched by the wall I found a piece of the bombshell. This piece must have fallen while I was there.

The baby carriage was loaded up with the two smallest children: Theresa, not yet one year old, and Gert, two and a half, as well as what overnight clothing would fit in. We all carried something, mostly clothes and some blankets, before making the one-kilometer walk to my aunt and uncle's. They owned a bedding and clothing store which was attached to their house. My parents were given the bedroom of one of their sons, Jan, who was going to share a room with my grandfather. Gert and Theresa slept in the room with my parents. The four older sisters, including me, were put up in cots, two on each level in the hallways.

As it turned out, we stayed there for six weeks and celebrated my birthday there. My friend Riekie came to visit and as a birthday present she gave me a chicken egg, which was very special. My mother fixed it for me alone, soft boiled. It was delicious. During the war we normally only had egg powder omelets because eggs were not available in stores and difficult to get from farmers.

Later we found out that the bombing raid was meant for the destruction of a railroad to prevent the Germans from transporting goods to Germany. They had missed the target, bombing several homes and killing three people.

We had a short wave radio

Nan Casey

My parents lived in Zeist, but I was working in Utrecht. We did not think it would be too bad in the beginning. Of course there was the blackout, rationing, handing in radios and gold and silver. Our coffee and tea was taken to Germany. My Dad even had to take our dog to a place to see if he was the right kind to be sent to the Russian front. He came back, thank goodness.

People kept disappearing. Some escaped to England to join the fighting. Lots of young men were sent to Germany to work, and later older men as well. My sister married her fiancé; they had a little girl in 1942. He was a manager in a big garage in Zeist. He was sent to Germany but after four months working for Lufthansa he came home on leave. He did not like working for the Nazis so he joined the Resistance instead. He had forged papers and we didn't see too much of him any more.

We often had young men coming to the store; then my Dad contacted someone, and subsequently they went to their hiding places in the countryside. Three operators In Utrecht were fired from the post office and taken away. They never came back. It was just a terrible time. We had a short wave radio, hidden of course, and we listened to news and speeches by the Queen and Churchill, and coded messages for the Resistance.

In Zeist there was no bombing, but in Utrecht we had air raid warnings. We would stop working, and spent a lot of time in the basement of the building.

One of the chores was standing in line

Lisette de Groot

When war broke out, our family lived in a small town not far from The Hague and Leiden, where my father was stationed in the Dutch army. By September of 1944 we lived with my grandmother in a big house near Arnhem. It had seemed safer to move there from the western part of the country, closer to the farms and food supply. That month was the big attempt by the Allied forces to conquer Arnhem, which lies on the Rhine River. From our kitchen window we watched hundreds of parachutists coming down. Even though a big battle lay ahead, we anticipated liberation in a few days.

However, it was not to be, and everyone was immensely disappointed. The Germans were not giving up; Arnhem was practically destroyed and its people had been evacuated right before the start of the fighting. Our house was filled with evacuees, relatives from Arnhem. Soon, however, the Germans ordered everyone to leave town, except for my other grandmother who was allowed to stay because of her age. It was a desolate sight to see them leave, parents walking with small children and few belongings. Where would they find a place to stay?

After the disappointment of the failed liberation attempt, followed by the separation from our relatives, a feeling of desolation set in. The household chores of day to day living kept everyone busy. All schools were closed now, but after some time about ten or twelve children were given daily lessons in preparation for the eventual return to school, which for us was going to be in the seventh Grade. We met in a room at the local gas factory at first, then in the garage of the doctor whose son was in our class. It was fortunate that the teacher was willing to do this, although the parents probably paid him in food or cash.

Now and then our village was attacked by projectiles shot from tanks. My father had instructed me on how to protect myself. "When you hear the boom, boom, boom in the distance", he said, "you have to listen to the direction of the sound, so that if the building gets hit, the wall will protect you instead of falling on you."

Sure enough, one day while walking to the gas factory for our classes, I heard the dreaded boom, boom, boom sound, like distant thunder. Quickly I ran to the other side of the street, lying down flat on the ground against the wall of a big building. More children and adults came and did the same thing. We were scared, but the bombs did not fall in that street but a couple of blocks away. Meanwhile I had to move over to make room for others, until I was almost with my nose in a dog's droppings.

One of the chores in those days was standing in line for bread or milk. The milk by then was very thin and bluish looking. Everyone came with his own container. Sometimes after standing in line for a long time, the milk supply would have run out by the time our turn came. I remember one time very clearly. My mother was pregnant and sent me to go for milk. Everyone waited patiently and made small talk. Suddenly the storekeeper announced, "Anyone who is pregnant may come to the head of the line." Immediately I went to the front, and the whole line of people roared with laughter. Here was this eleven-year-old trying to get ahead of them! All I could do was mumble that it was my mother who was pregnant. I had to go back to my place in line.

One thing I learned during the war that lying or hiding the truth from the enemy is permissible when you have to protect yourself. At other times a lie would result in punishment.

They were Christians!

Rita Binder

During the winter of 1944-45, my mother went to some farmers in hopes of getting food. She came across a group of Germans having lunch in a barn. To her astonishment she witnessed a German stand up and say Grace. On her arrival home she exclaimed, "The Germans are Christians!"
We thought all Germans were 'godless'.

The ammunition exploded

Martha Gubbels

I was 7 years old, living in Liessel in the province of Brabant, when the Germans invaded The Netherlands on May 10, 1940. I did not see any fighting as far as I can remember. It seemed the Germans had just walked into our country, but we soon found out that it was not that simple.

As time went by the Germans changed the laws, something that was not very well accepted by the Dutch population. We had ration coupons for most of our food. These coupons were traded almost like currency for other things that people wanted. The farm where we lived provided enough food for a family of ten. For a while a young man who was from the northern part of The Netherlands and who was hiding from the Germans, stayed with us as well. The local farmers took in these young men who escaped the German work camps in Liessel, because they were afraid they might be sent to Germany.

My oldest brother Harry, coming home from work in the neighboring town of Asten, met up with some people who had found a box of ammunition. Fortunately, my brother did not hang around, because the box of ammunition exploded killing eight people and wounding thirteen. He returned to help the wounded and put body parts together for the families of the dead. For years this incident has been difficult for him to think about.

We were liberated for the first time September 23, 1944. I

remember the fighting seemed not that heavy somehow. The soldiers were coming into town in big tanks, handing out chocolates and crackers to the children, and cigarettes to the adults. The Germans retreated to a swampy area and strengthened their forces. For weeks they shot missiles into the town, damaging the local Catholic church and other buildings, wounding some, and killing others. In the last days of October, the Germans were back in full force. We had to pack up and leave our home to go to Asten were it was safe. My dad said we were lucky because we were all together and we were all okay.

I remember a family of eighteen who were trying to leave their home and three of the children were killed, some were wounded, and I believe the German military doctor looked after them. Fighting became heavy in our area, with American and British soldiers fighting against the Germans. One of my cousins, who stayed behind in Liessel with some neighbors, said that at times the whole town looked like it was on fire. Two-thirds of the town and the surrounding area were destroyed. Scottish soldiers who fought one on one with the Germans, and were backed up by British tanks eventually liberated our area. Many, many died. It has been said that the Liessel area saw the worst fighting after Normandy.

I lost three cousins in the war. One was a policeman who was transporting English-speaking men, British or American pilots. German officers stopped them, and my cousin was shot when these men spoke. Another cousin was sent to a concentration camp in Germany, and returned alive in 1945. He told his mother that the hunger was the worst, and he died of malnutrition shortly afterwards in Groningen. His sister died in a car accident during liberation festivities in Helmond, where she was working.

My family returned, without me and three of my siblings, to find that everything had been destroyed by fire. I was sent to another city, Helmond, to live with an aunt and uncle for nine months. The three other siblings lived with another uncle and aunt in Westerhoven for six months.

Forty-eight years later, in 1992, I returned to Liessel from Canada for a visit. I attended the opening of a World War II monument in honor of the liberators and the local people who had died. Two of my cousins are remembered on this monument, and twenty-one Scottish people were there to receive the honour.

'Dirty' eyes

Adriana Lyffyt

I was born in 1941 and spent most of my years as a baby and toddler away from my parents who lived in Rotterdam. They did Underground work such as hiding Jewish people and shipping them to England, while I was living with a German family (which was ironic) on a river barge on the Rhine till the end of the war, as one of them.

I vividly remember German soldiers coming on board all the time to check what was in the cargo hold. I remember that at eye level I would see the high boots they wore, and that they would pick me up and comment on me being a towhead with white-blond hair, but also on my brown eyes, which was not so good in their opinion. They said my eyes were a little dirty. Other than that they were very gentle young men. The people who had taken me in to save my life in case my parents should get caught, were angels. We all survived the war, but I never again saw the 'angels' who risked their lives to save mine. I regret that.

Visiting the redhead

Minie Kerstholt

My father did a lot for the prisoners in the Vught camp, as well as for those in other camps where Dutch people had been sent. He provided food, and maintained contact as much as possible with the Underground. At home we had several people in hiding, and we also stored Jewish Bibles and clothing belonging to our Jewish neighbours. My brother was hiding on a farm in Winterswijk where he could make himself useful, and in that way escape the Germans.

Hoogezand-Sappemeer, where we lived, was full of N.S.B. guys, traitors. We had the N.S.B. mayor living right next door to us, and he knew of my brother's existence. Someone betrayed my brother, and he was picked up in Winterswijk. From there he landed in a work camp in Germany, where he was badly mistreated. He ended up in a hospital and died at the age of nineteen. My father reproached himself and within a year he died too.

My sister Ans was a nurse in the Academic Hospital at Groningen. That city was bombed and all patients and nurses had to be evacuated. They landed in trenches half full of water, the nurses malnourished and overworked, with tuberculosis patients in their care. It was a dangerous situation, and as a result, five of the nurses contracted TB. In those days the cure for TB was lots of fresh air and years in a sanatorium.

Liberation eventually came, and Canadian soldiers had to get a medical checkup at the hospital. They made friends with the sick nurses and tossed magazines, chocolate and cigarettes over the fence of the sanatorium. My sister had red hair, and one of the soldiers asked the supervising nurse if he could visit the redhead. He got permission, and for a number of years they corresponded regularly, resulting first in friendship and then love. Even though my sister was still sick, the Canadian refused to give up, and though his future wife had to continue her cure he came over twice from Canada to pay her a visit. Not till 1950 was she well enough to come to Canada.

Every night
we packed the baby carriage

Jacoba J. Bessey

Dad owned a truck, which he had used to deliver building materials around the country. Shortly after the German occupation began, the Nazis confiscated his truck and made him work as a mechanic in their garages. In retaliation he occasionally sabotaged their trucks by putting sugar in the gas tanks. When caught, he spent one and a half years in jail for that, but they could as easily have shot him on the spot. In October of 1943 my dad was allowed to visit his family for a week. It was nice because until then we didn't know if he was dead or alive. It was great to have him home, but soon he had to go back to France to resume his duties for the German army. We tried to make the best of it.

We had rations but they were pretty skimpy. We were allowed extra milk for the two youngest, who were now two and four years old. As I look back on it I have to admire my mother for keeping the family going. The oldest was seventeen and the youngest was two and a half. Every night we packed the baby carriage with whatever food we had and clothes for everyone, and left it by the front door in case we had to run for shelter during an air strike.

On April 16, 1943, the Allies tried to destroy the rail works in Haarlem but mistook a schoolyard for the rail yard and bombed our neighbourhood instead. Houses all around us were destroyed, and one hundred and twenty people died that day. It was a scary experience but we were very lucky and survived the day unscathed. Christmas 1943 was very bleak. My grandfather brought over a wild rabbit for us and it made a delicious Christmas dinner. There were no presents but we had this wonderful German lady next door whose children were fully-grown. She unraveled their old woolen sweaters and knitted mittens for us. She was married to a Jewish tailor, and even though of German blood, she hated the Nazis as much as, if not more than, the rest of us. Sadly, when the Nazis collected all the Jewish citizens from our neighbourhood, she stuck by her family and went to the death camp with them. Two of her children survived it, but we never saw the woman or her husband again. We saved some of their furniture for when the children returned. The sad part is that I can't even remember their names.

It was about this time that my mother found out she was pregnant again, and she was very sick. We worried about her health and about what would become of our future if she did not survive. My oldest sister was working for the Resistance, carrying messages and news bulletins from the Allies. I remember my mother waiting by the front door right at curfew time, waiting to hear the familiar tune my sister used to whistle when she walked.

On one occasion, my other sister, Ann, came across a terrible scene. It turned out that a German soldier had been shot and the troops were questioning the crowd of onlookers. When no one confessed to the crime, the soldiers took a group of citizens and executed them right in front of her. This was a tactic used by the Nazis to put fear in our minds, and it worked very well.

We lived close to the national railway centre in Haarlem and lots of our neighbours worked there. The Germans used the railroad to transport food and ammunition to their troops, and to take away our art treasures. Word came from England through the Resistance that all railroad workers should go on strike and then into hiding. The Germans were furious and staged razzias, raids. They closed off our neighbourhood and searched every house for men and boys, and took them to concentration camps.

On June 6, 1944 (D-Day), the Allies landed in France. We thought that Belgium and Holland, being so small, would be liberated in a week. Boy, were we wrong. Dad was in Lille, France, and we had not heard from him in months. Phones were non-existent and the mail was very sporadic. We listened to the radio as often as we dared and heard there was fierce fighting in France. We could only pray for his safe return home.

June 8 was my parents' 19th wedding anniversary. Mom and some neighbours were listening to the BBC while my sister Ann and I watched for German soldiers. A man came to our front door and we yelled for everyone to put the radio away. We thought it was the Gestapo, but Mom looked out of the window and recognized the familiar face in an instant. We hadn't seen Dad for so long that we barely recognized him. He told us stories of the Allied troops, the tanks, the flamethrowers and the fighting, and all he'd been able to think of was to just find a way home. He told us he had stolen a truck from the Germans that was full of ammunition and drove it through Belgium. He knew some people in Brussels where he left the truck for the Resistance. They helped him cross the Dutch border and he made his way home. I guess the excitement was too much for my mother. She went into labour and at 3 a.m. Dad took her to the hospital. There were no cabs or cars of any kind, so he put her on the back of his bicycle and walked her to the hospital about twenty minutes away. They had to cross a bridge that was guarded by German soldiers. They gave them a little trouble because no one was allowed on the street after curfew, but one look at Mom and they let her pass. Early in the morning we got the cutest and tiniest baby sister, Tina, who weighed only three and a half pounds. Mom didn't think the baby would survive and had her baptized right away. She was a tough one though. Today she is in her fifties, married, with four grownup children and living in Ottawa.

School started in September, but even that was difficult. There was very little paper, and pencils were hard to find. They brought back the slates, and a special crayon made of slate called a griffel. The school tried to stay open but as the weather turned colder, we only went for half days.

I was warm in this outfit

Nelia Barnfield

I was only two at the beginning of the war. We were living in Enschede. The German bombers on their way to England flew over our house quite low. I would scream "Chine fly! Chine fly!" – machine fly – and come running into the house. For a long time after the war I could not look at pictures of planes.

I remember the horrible, sickly smell in our living room of sugar beets simmering in a large pan on our potbelly stove. We wrapped up a pot of hutspot (potatoes and carrots mashed together) in newspapers and blankets to cook the ingredients. I became anemic at age six, which became a problem for years to come.

One year I wore unlined rain boots and developed terrible chilblains. My heels were purple. I also had a pair of wooden shoes, which I wore out totally. One day I was late for school because snow had made a pointed ice ball under the soles, so that I could barely walk.

In 1941 we had moved to Leiden. Opposite our house was a wooden pedestrian bridge across the canal. During the previous winter some of the boards had been cut out during the night to be used for firewood making the bridge unusable.

During my year in second grade we missed much school. There was no fuel to heat the buildings. It was arranged with another school to heat only one building at a time, which meant classes for only half a day. Our teacher was fantastic because she had us all come to her house, about three children at a time, to recite our times tables.

My mother, who was an accomplished seamstress, made me a winter coat with a hood and matching pants. Out of desperation she used velvet drapes for the fabric, and for the lining, an old dressing gown. I was very warm in this outfit.

They were shot down like flies

John Keulen

I spent a lot of time with my friend Berend Nagelhout. He was the oldest son of a very poor family with seven or eight children. They lived a little ways out of the town of Bakhuizen where I lived, on a hill called Witland (white land), a cluster of about four houses on a dirt road. In 1944 we were both thirteen years old, and I often visited him at his house, which was very small for such a large family. There was no indoor plumbing. All the children slept in the loft under the exposed tile roof. There were no separate bedrooms. Most slept on the floor or on thin mattresses, with boys and girls separated by some sheets or gunnysacks hanging from the rafters. During winter storms snow would blow through cracks in the tile roof, and cover the children's blankets and faces. During heavy rains, pails had to be placed at strategic points.

Berend's father Hans was an itinerant laborer who took employment wherever he could find it. Still, it was a happy family, that always shared with me the little they had. One of the father's proudest possessions was his large Philips radio, which so far he had managed to keep out of German hands by refusing to turn it in. He loved to listen to the Dutch BBC broadcasts from England to keep abreast of the war news. The house being very small, there was a lack of good hiding places, and a mere perfunctory search would soon have disclosed the location of the radio.

On a Saturday afternoon when I was visiting Berend's house, it was reported that two Landwachters, Dutch traitors, were chasing a young man who had been in hiding, and that they were close by. Berend's father told Berend to dig a deep hole in the garden as fast as he could. Two other sons were posted as lookouts.

Meanwhile Hans wrapped his prized radio in some old gunnysacks, and was carrying it out of the house toward the hole Berend had just dug. At that instant one of the lookouts hollered, "They are coming!" I had given Berend a hand digging a four foot deep hole in the soft sandy soil. His father arrived with the radio, popped it into the hole without further ado, and frantically started filling it in. He was barely finished, when we heard gunshots. One of the Landwachters suddenly jumped out of the bushes with a smoking gun in his hand. "Where is my partner," he screamed.

"We haven't seen anybody," Hans nervously answered with the spade still in his hand. The man disappeared again, running, still after his prey. Severely shaken, Hans smoothed the last few shovels of dirt, planted some flowers in the fresh soil, and went back into the house. The radio was dug up after the war, but it never played again.

When a flurry of German activity started in the middle of September 1944, we knew something big was afoot. German officers went to and fro in their cars, and large trucks with enormous canvas covered loads entered the woods and came out empty. German sentries surrounded the square kilometer of forested area, and no civilians were allowed in. My uncle Ypke and his family, who lived in the woods, were forced to leave.

Long, cigar shaped objects started arriving on long truck beds, covered by tarps.

Then in the evening of Monday, September 25, at exactly 7.00 p.m. we were startled by a loud roar. It was dusk and we had just finished supper. We rushed outside in time to see a giant rocket with its bright fiery tail pushing skyward and rapidly gaining speed. Never having seen or heard of such a phenomenon, we were totally baffled and afraid. The two University of Delft students, who were hiding with my family, were better informed. Having studied various propulsion systems at the university, they correctly deduced that this must be one of the 'retaliatory weapons' with which Hitler had promised to wipe out England.

Soon BBC Radio confirmed that London was indeed the target of the V-2s, but many did not reach the city and fell on thinly populated areas. It was impossible to intercept these weapons, and their arrival could not be predicted. Even though V-2s did little damage, they must have caused much anxiety among the British populace.

As a boy, I was already very interested in facts and figures, and I kept meticulous records of all the V-2 launchings. The Germans launched seventy-six V-2s from our area. Not all were successful. On three of them the rocket motor stopped soon after launch, and the V-2s plummeted back to earth and exploded.

I was eyewitness to one of these from about one mile away. For almost one hour I had been waiting for a launch from a good vantage point. My patience was finally rewarded as I saw the V-2 climb above the trees. It must have been about one mile high when the bright glow at the tail suddenly extinguished. The V-2 stopped in midair in slow motion, and started falling earthward faster and faster in total silence. I saw a bright flash as it exploded upon impact. The combination of a full load of liquid oxygen, plus the warhead, caused a gigantic crater and uprooted a sizable portion of forest, but no casualties were reported. The explosion caused many broken windows in Bakhuizen and nearby villages.

On most days four or five V-2s were launched, with six per day as the maximum. The logistics of transporting the V-2s were no small matter. The narrow roads through many Dutch towns were a nightmare for the German trucks with their long loads. In the town of Balk they had to back up several times to negotiate an extremely tight corner. An eyewitness at that location told me the V-2 must have been loaded with liquid oxygen already, as icicles were hanging from the truck and this was late September with still fairly warm weather. The Germans must have had two launching platforms, as numbers 35 and 36 were launched within two minutes of each other. After almost one month of ceaseless V-2 activity, it suddenly stopped with the launch of number 76 at 10.40 a.m. on Friday, October 20, 1944. The Germans pulled out with all their equipment in a matter of hours, and it became eerily quiet. Now only the drone of the bombers on their regular bombing runs filled the sky.

Why did the Germans leave in such a hurry? Their espionage channels must have been better than we gave them credit for. The next day six British Mosquito fighter-bombers strafed the V-2 launching site in low altitude runs, but there was not a German around, and the British effort didn't cause a single casualty.

By 1944, the war had lasted over four years, and fuel of all types was scarce. This included coal, the primary fuel for the large pumping stations on the shores of the IJssel Lake. These pumping stations controlled the water levels within the province of Friesland. They stood idle throughout the coal shortage, and could not pump the excess water into the IJssel Lake. The result was that large areas frequently flooded during periods of heavy rain.

Then winter weather set in, and the flooded areas froze over. This was a boon for ice skating enthusiasts, which included virtually all Frisians. Ice-skating races and other winter sport events were immediately organized, and I remember these were some of the most enjoyable times during those bleak war years. Bakhuizen had a very active skating club. Both my grandfather, Sjoerd Deden, and Klaas van der Weij, my future father-in-law, were on the board of directors.

Skating events on the shallow flooded areas could be held much earlier than on the larger lakes and were much safer as the water under the ice was only inches deep. Our neighbor, Yme van der Wal, always prepared a hundred liters or so of hot chocolate milk, plus snacks, which he took to the races on a sled and sold out of a tent he set up on the ice. I still remember how good his hot chocolate tasted on a cold winter afternoon. Yme had a large family, and being a vegetable grower, had no income during the winter months.

During the course of the war about eighty planes were shot down over southwest Friesland alone, an area of about twenty square miles. Most were British or American, but twenty of them were German planes. I have personal recollections of a number of these crashes and visited their sites as a boy. During the 1980s I met an old RCAF flier in California who had been shot down over Friesland in 1942. We got talking and I was able to piece together an amazing story. His name was Bernie Pilgrim, and he was a radio man. In the night of July 27, 1942, his two-engine Wellington had made a bombing mission to Hamburg. On the plane's return it was attacked by two German fighters and in a matter of seconds the plane's centre section caught fire. The plane rapidly lost altitude and the pilot gave the order to bail out as he could not keep the plane in the air much longer. Bernie was the second man to jump, after tail gunner Rondeau. The navigator, Thorpe, was the last man able to parachute out. Bombardier Brogan, who had helped Pilgrim fight the fire, had to return to the cockpit for his parachute. He never made it and rode the plane down with pilot Mason who stayed at the controls. Three men saved, two lost, and this was only their second mission of the required thirty.

As Pilgrim hit the ground he saw the bright explosion of the Wellington in the distance as the burning plane hit the waters of IJssel Lake. He had barely landed on solid ground, while Thorpe wound up in the water but could swim to shore. They were in an empty wasteland, which turned out to be the Northeast Polder under construction. The three survivors found refuge for the rest of the night in a pile of building materials. In the morning they were spotted by a German patrol and taken to Lemmer for interrogation. Eventually they were transported to prisoner-of-war camp Stalag Luft lll in Sagan, western Poland. They built an escape tunnel, and eighty men escaped before the plot was discovered. All but a few were recaptured and fifty were executed. Bernie Pilgrim owed his life to the fact that, although he had helped build the tunnel, he had been transferred to another camp just before the escape. British forces liberated him in May 1945 near Lübeck, Germany, after almost three years in captivity.

In 1985 when I visited Friesland, I learned that fishermen had retrieved a piece of airplane wreckage which turned out to be a piece of Bernie's Wellington, forty-three years after it was shot down. I obtained a small portion of the wreck and took it to Bernie in California. He was overcome with emotion, and with tears in his eyes said, "We really didn't have a chance. We were shot down like flies." Upon investigation I found out that thirty-two British planes failed to return that night, and Bernie's squadron lost 23% of its planes. That was four times the 'acceptable rate' for plane losses. They were indeed shot down like flies.

All the cemeteries in the villages around us bore testimony to British, American, Australian, New Zealand, and even Polish fliers whose lives had come to an untimely end. When Germans were shot down they were generally transported to Germany for military funerals.

A flying bomb

Johanna Opdam

We lived in Lisse, near the Lijnden Woods that belong to a castle there. One night in September of 1944 a thunderous noise woke us up, and everyone thought a bomb had been dropped by British planes. The next day all the neighbours were talking on the street about the noise, but no one knew what had happened. That night we went to bed at 11.00 p.m. hoping for a good sleep. But no, at two in the morning the same loud noise woke us up. We were all terribly frightened.

This continued every night until one of our neighbours, a woman of German background, went to talk to a German soldier. She found out that a machine in the woods was shooting V-2 rockets to England. The soldier explained that this was a flying bomb shot from the woods, and that Italian soldiers were being used to do the job. As they caught fire every time they shot a rocket, they had dug a deep hole, filled with water, and they jumped into this hole to extinguish the flames. Some died in the process.

They said it was an Allied air raid

Frank VanderKley

Our family was living in the Hazelaar Street in The Hague. If you looked northward down the street during the fall of 1944 you could see the V-2 rockets being fired and rising above the houses on Valkenboschkade. The sight was frightening, and there was a tremendous noise accompanied by a fiery tail. We watched the rockets climb and turn westwards. Everybody would heave a sigh of relief when they started their journey across the North Sea. We did not think of damage or possible victims on the far side, where the rocket would come down. But once in a while the firing or steering mechanism would fail and the rocket would fall back or take an unintended course.

On New Year's Day that was exactly what happened. I was standing near the back window on the third floor of our house, looking eastward. I had my hands on the windowpane and was looking out, because there was a tremendous whistling sound almost right overhead, and I tried to see where it came from. I felt the windowpane bulge, but it did not break. The rocket whistled overhead like a black shadow. It fell somewhere behind the Kamperfoelie church. There was a loud explosion and everyone started running to see what had happened. The large windowpane of the grocery store at the corner had come out of its frame, and stood beside the gaping hole as if a giant had set it there.

I ran out of the house. My grandmother lived in the direction where the rocket had come down. There was panic in the streets. Less than a thousand meters farther the bomb had hit a block of houses with disastrous consequences. My grandmother was not hurt. If the V-2 had only landed two hundred meters further on it would have hit either the school gardens or the cemetery and done minimal damage. Soon a German platoon was cordoning off the disaster area and we were told that this had been a bomb attack by the Allies and that we should go home.

That block of houses has since been rebuilt and there is a plaque in one wall commemorating the event.

Memory glimpses
from the last year of the war

Enno Reckendorf

During summer vacation, I tied sheaves of rye on a nearby farm that served as a youth hostel. After harvest I camped with a friend near Oldenzaal, visiting girl campers. Returned to our tent long after curfew, loudly singing German songs to avoid arrest. Returning home, found that Mother and Sis had gone to Amsterdam into hiding. I was to join them by train.

Then, the railroad strike. No electricity, no gas in Amsterdam, or anywhere. Soup kitchen's daily dole. Went to Utrecht by canal boat with wood-gas generator, at night to avoid strafing. Walked to Bilthoven to Kees Boeke's school. Few lessons, mostly bargaining and begging in countyrside for apples, potatoes, eggs. December, walked to Amsterdam on an empty stomach. Somehow Mother finagled Christmas eve passage on a German night train for us, two nights to go 100 kilometers. Christmas day in Amersfoort during a bombing raid. Arrived in Zwolle late that night, went to friends' house near station. Surprise: next door Father was in hiding. Happy, brief reunion.

Walked to Dalfsen to go into hiding with family of hardware store owner. Spent much time helping to obtain food from farms. New Year's Eve 1944: no oliebollen! At midnight a huge noise: a V-2 launched from the nearby Rechteren estate. Many more followed in the next two months. Saw some fall back on the launch pad.

Early March returned home as Mr. Hardware made advances on Mother. On my 15th birthday had picture taken for ID card. Paper seal which fixed photo to card was needed by Underground for fake ID. My seal was fake.

Our subsistence farming neighbour was called up for transport duty with horse and wagon. I went in his stead and transferred a crate of artillery shells from train to ammo dump in familiar woods. Passive resistance: all the horses in 'low gear' all day.

Sitting on the front bumper of a truck

Harm Duursma

By 1944 there was a severe lack of food, clothing, and just about everything else. One afternoon in August of that year, some other men and I were on the roof of the Dickers foundry in Hengelo where I worked to black out some windows. I had to come down to pick up something from the shop. When I arrived at the shop I saw a group of German soldiers stop at the gate of the factory, placing a machine gun there. I quickly told the other men to stay where they were and removed the ladder. When I got back to the shop I joined some men who were hiding in a closet. While we were in there, we heard lots of shouting inside the building and heard the soldiers ordering men to go outside. So we decided we should go outside as well.

We were lined up in rows of four. I saw lots of women who had come to the steel fence in front of the building. I recognized my wife holding up a parcel and asking one of the young soldiers standing near me if he would give the parcel to me. He told me I could go and get it, and with the rifle in my back I was allowed to go to my wife. She handed me my parcel and I returned to the line I had been in. The parcel contained half a loaf of bread - all the bread she had at home - and a sweater. We were made to walk to the railroad station where we waited till midnight to board a train.

While on the train we came to a sudden stop because

the Dutch Resistance had removed a portion of the rails. A replacement engine was hooked onto the back of the train and we returned to Hengelo. Then our train took us on another track. That time the train had to stop because of an air raid. We learned that an ammunition train was under attack, so we fled from the train and found a place to hide. When the air raid was over we were escorted back to the train with fewer men, as several had made an escape. This kind of thing happened twice more before we actually got to the city of Zwolle. We were taken to a school where we slept on straw.

The next morning, after a couple of sandwiches, we were taken to just outside the city to dig a canal. This was to prevent the Allied troops from entering the city. At noon a large container of hot meals was delivered; however we had no plates or utensils. We cleaned the dirt off our shovels, loaded the food on them, and fashioned forks from small tree branches.

Because I had injured my thumb, the doctor advised I needed a few days' rest and I was allowed to go home for five days. With no transportation available, I walked until 8 p.m. and asked for shelter at a farm. They allowed me to stay overnight in a haystack, high above ground. When I woke up in the morning, the ladder had been removed. After a while I saw the farmer coming out of the house and walking in the other direction. After a while he returned with the ladder and said I could come down. I started to leave but he insisted I come in and have a good breakfast.

I thanked my hosts and started out because I still had fifty kilometers to go. After three or four hours walking, a German truck came along and offered me a ride. Taking a chance, I accepted. A few kilometers from my destination the truck took a different direction, so I jumped off, landed on the road, and walked home. My wife was very happy to have me there for a few days.

After my sick leave I returned to the base, but the Germans soon sent me back to work at the Dickers factory. This time the trip was made while sitting on the front bumper of a transport truck.

The city of Hengelo was liberated on April 12, 1945.

A plate
of sauerkraut and bacon

Henry van Ommen

In February of 1945, we had one day that was about the coldest of that winter. During the morning the entire town found itself surrounded by German soldiers. Everywhere you looked you saw guards keeping watch. They had come to capture men for work on the IJssel defense line. Everyone was shut in, and every house was searched. In those days they were always holding raids to capture men.

At our house, four men were caught in the trap: My father, an uncle, and two neighbours were trapped in our house, and were discussing how to escape.

Mother had just put a big pan of food on the table, sauerkraut and bacon. I quickly asked her for a plate of food, for the guard behind our house. We had two hayricks behind the house, and a little farther on there were two concrete silos about two meters high. If the German guard stood behind the silos, he could get out of the nasty eastern wind a bit, but couldn't see what was happening in the house. The poor guy didn't even have a warm coat on.

When I gave him the sauerkraut dinner he came out of the wind quickly enough. This allowed the four men to escape across a deep ditch behind the house, with the ice thick enough for them to walk on. With the soldier occupied elsewhere, it didn't take them long to escape into the polder.

They faced the firing squad

Richard Oostra

As the war continued, and the Germans were experiencing major military losses, they took over our school to house the wounded. This meant we couldn't go to school anymore. As kids we considered this to be a bonus.

You learned to steal bags full of coal, something that was no longer available to us, but of which the Germans had plenty in their storage places. Food from the farms was shipped by trainloads to Germany while many Dutch citizens went hungry. We did not consider lying to, or stealing from, the Germans a sin, because we did not consider them our legally elected government. They were our oppressors, killing innocent people and robbing our resources.

We had a cousin from Amsterdam living with us. He had forged papers indicating that he was in the German navy. One day I was with him and two German soldiers stopped him to ask for his identity papers. When he showed them, they both stood at attention for him. We jumped on our bikes again and went on our way.

My father worked on the railroad, and they were asked by the Dutch government in England to go on strike in order to slow German transportation of equipment. Going on strike could mean the death penalty if you were caught. In the railroad station in our city is a monument with the names of several of my father's co-workers who got caught and faced the firing squad. One day the Gestapo came to our house looking for my father. We told them he was not at home, but he was hiding in my bedroom. That was scary for me as a boy, but it made us feel part of the war effort. We also saw Jewish people forced into boxcars, even children, being shipped to Germany. We didn't know where they were going until we learned, after the war, that they had all been killed in the gas chambers.

After D-Day our city jail was filled with a lot of Resistance men who had been caught. One night what appeared to be a German military truck arrived, pretending to bring in more prisoners. Once inside, the guards found that they had been fooled, and that the truck was driven by resistance fighters, who forced them to release all the political prisoners. The guards themselves were put in the cells. The next morning our city swarmed with German Gestapo who searched every house for escaped prisoners but none were found. One family near us had three sons who were also in the Resistance movement but had been caught. They and several other men were shot in a field nearby our home just two weeks before the Germans surrendered.

They were singing the national anthem

John Looyenga

I was born in Bozum, a town in Friesland of about five hundred people, where my parents had lived for more than twenty years. My Dad, Aan Looyenga had a freight transport business. During the war, some farmers who had relatives in the city sometimes asked Dad if he was willing to take them a few bottles of milk and some food. The Germans did not allow this. Dad put a long black stovepipe on the wagon and fitted some bottles of milk in there. That way the Germans did not get suspicious. Part of Dad's business was dealing in coal; therefore it was not uncommon for them to have stovepipes and coal as part of the freight.

One time he had a coffin on his wagon, filled with food sent by the farmers to their families. The Germans did not want to open a coffin and the food was delivered safely. One other day, when my father had left an hour later than usual, he returned with everything still on the wagon. About five kilometers before his destination, people had warned him that the Germans were stopping all traffic and took everything they had. So Dad turned around and took everything back home.

Another time the Germans stopped him and demanded that he go to their headquarters. He went there; they took everything off the wagon but, thankfully, they allowed him to keep his horse and wagon.

My brother Bert and I often accompanied Dad when

carting freight to Leeuwarden. Usually we went along just to make sure no one robbed the load while Dad was taking care of the business dealings. That was plenty of responsibility for a nine-year-old during wartime.

Dad and his partner, Nelis Dijkstra, once bought a 1934 Ford truck. The Germans always stole whatever they wanted without any consideration. When they stole the truck, Dad thought they would never see it again, but after the war he learned that it had been found at an airbase near Leeuwarden. When he picked it up, it was still in good running condition and we were able to use it again.

The Reformed church at Bozum had a clock tower where people used to keep watch to see if any Germans were approaching the town. In that case they would blow a horn as a warning to the townspeople. .

There were two bells in the church tower. Both of these had been made in France in 1633. The Germans stole the bells and I watched as they loaded them on the trucks and drove away. I knew that there was a good chance that the bells would be melted down and the metal used for military purposes. After the war, however, the larger bell was identified and returned to the town of Bozum but the smaller one was never seen again. As a temporary measure, a cart wheel was hung in the tower in the place of the small bell. It hung there until March 15, 1976, when the church received a small bell weighing 690 kilos from a Roman Catholic Church in Rotterdam that had been torn down.

As a young woman, my mother had worked for the headmaster of the Reformed school in Rinsumageest. The headmaster's son, Pieter Glastra van Loon, was in hiding on a farm during the tail end of the war. At the same farm there was also a German man in hiding who was supposed to work for the Wehrmacht, but wanted nothing to do with National Socialism. In February of 1945 both were picked up, along with four other Resistance workers who had also been in hiding. All were tortured and then executed in a farmer's field. I remember hearing that, even after the torture, they were singing the Wilhelmus, the Dutch national anthem, as they were being shot. The shooting had been in retaliation for a Resistance attack on Grietje Sinnema, a Frisian girl who had worked as an interpreter for the Germans. Pieter Glastra van Loon's wife was pregnant at the time he was killed; she had a son eight months later and named him after his father.

At the end of the war the Resistance cut down all the trees along the roads near Bozum, and placed them across the roads to prevent the Germans from using these roads. Shortly after the war it was decided to plant new trees to replace the ones that had been cut down. This job was given to local school kids to do as a project, with the thinking that if the kids planted a tree, and if they were proud of their job, they wouldn't damage the young trees as they grew. A little past Schuurman's house is a dairy farm and just a little past that on the right hand side is the tree that I planted. I can still pick out the tree I planted so long ago. I also still know the names of most of the people who lived in Bozum when I was young.

I did not know this man

Marijke Shaban

My memories of the war are few, as I was only four years and a few months old when the war ended. I was sent to the soup kitchen, wearing wooden shoes. The snow used to stick to the soles, which made walking difficult. Mother needed to stay home with the three brothers who were born after me.

I remember sitting on the only large chair in the house, in the dark, rocking back and forth, lamenting, and wondering when the lights would come back on.

My father was in the Resistance movement and away for long periods of time. When he did come home I hid under the table because I did not know this man and wanted nothing to do with him. He must have been home near the end of the war, as I remember us all hanging out of the attic window and marveling at the food parcels that were being dropped by the allies.

Little did we know...

Anne Hendren

On clear nights Britain's Royal Air Force was heavily bombing the Ruhr and Rhine regions in Germany, targeting the ammunition factories. Hundreds of bombers flew right across Holland and across Utrecht where we lived. Just as we had fallen asleep on those clear moonlit nights the air raid sirens would go off. We all scrambled to get dressed and go downstairs to sit around the living room table. We were so tired that we put our heads on the table and tried to sleep that way. We were lucky if we only had to get up once a night.

The Germans became more and more jumpy as they realized they might be losing the war, and would shoot at anything and anyone they thought looked suspicious. I had a near escape one time while riding my bicycle. It had wooden tires, as rubber was no longer available. On the way to school I tried to hit a friend biking in front of me with an apple core. My aim was slightly off and I hit a German soldier on the sidewalk instead!

The man looked furious but did not know where the apple had come from. With my heart beating like crazy I raced as fast as I could to get out of his line of sight.

On my mother's birthday on June 6, 1944, the Allied invasion to liberate Europe began on the coast of Normandy in France We were sitting outside in the late afternoon when our neighbour, a priest, rushed into our enclosed yard and excitedly gave us the news. We all became very emotional, jumping for joy, dancing and hugging and crying.

All of us were so full of high hopes, believing the war would be over in a matter of weeks. Some people picked flowers and stood at the entrance of the city waiting for the liberating forces to arrive. Little did we know that the worst part of the war was still to come, and we would be subject to almost another year of virtually unbearable misery and hardship.

Hand-me-downs

Cornelius Zaat

As food became more and more scarce, people began organizing soup kitchens. The food would be prepared by volunteers at a central place and from there distributed to different locations. At a certain time in the afternoon people would walk to this location with their dish or pan, and volunteers would scoop it up for the hungry crowd. My brother Gerry was one of the volunteers, dishing out a number of scoops depending on the size of the family. Sometimes he managed to get a little extra soup for the family to fight over, once the work was done.

The large metal containers with soup were transported by horse and wagon from the central kitchen to the co-op hall in our town, where it was handed out. The wagon would pass right by our house, and my younger brother Johnny and I had a trick to get more than our fair share even before it reached the co-op. We threw a stick of wood in front of the wagon wheels, one on each side, which made the wagon jump and spill soup all over the wooden floorboards. Then John and I would climb on the running wagon and lick up all the spilled food from the floor. Boy, oh boy, that tasted so-o-o good!

As children we learned at a very young age the value of items such as warm hand-me-downs from older siblings, and food. Wasting food was unacceptable and unheard of. As for the hand-me-downs, there was a lady in our town who was a very clever seamstress. She would do the more complicated sewing for our family, such as giving new life to an aging winter coat. The procedure was to take the coat apart at the seams, turn the pieces inside out and put it all back together again. We called it keren, which means to turn, and it gave the old coat many more years of service for the smaller Zaat kids.

As for wasting food, anything edible was considered a precious thing to keep us alive. We ate dog and cat meat, sugar beets, tulip bulbs, or black bread, one slice a day, no butter or margarine on it. We ate potatoes in the peel; nothing went to waste.

At one point, a strange dog would hang around our yard, looking for a little morsel. We noticed this animal coming back day after day, until one day he did not come back. The following day we had meat on our plate. Dad said it was rabbit, but we all knew better. We never asked him, just pretended to believe him. I was fourteen years old before I tasted bananas, oranges, peanuts, rice and many other food items for the first time.

Most people were more than happy to help out, but, unfortunately, there were also exceptions. These were mostly farming people who grew their own produce.

My sister Lydia worked for a farming family as a housemaid. Her wages were a warm meal a day. When my Dad was bed-ridden with hunger edema (caused by lack of proper food and vitamins,) my sister asked the farmer's wife if she was allowed to take home some left over potatoes that were meant to go to the pigs. The woman replied, "Well, just for once, but don't ever ask again."

On one occasion, my brother Johnny and I were walking, cold and hungry, through Wateringen, a town near Kwintsheul where we lived. We decided to go to a farmhouse and ask for something to eat; it didn't matter what. We knew these farming people and we also knew they would not give us anything. That was not in the plan. The people had a big dog and the woman always left a bowl of dog food on the back steps of the house.

I would go to the front door and ring the bell, the dog would react and come running to the front. The farmer's wife would answer the door and I would ask for something to eat, knowing she would turn me down. Meanwhile John would go to the back porch, steal the bowl of dog food and run off with it. Later, I would join him in a designated spot and we would clean out the bowl of dog food. Once it was empty, we sneaked back to the house and replaced the bowl on the steps.

However, these types of people were the exception. Most people were more than happy to help out where help was needed, at the risk of getting caught.

The four youngest ones of our family had what could be called a 'happy haven' where we could get a good solid meal several times a week. Of the four of us, my sister Nellie and I were the best off. About kitty-corner from our house was a bakery shop where fresh bread was being baked. They had orders to provide for the Wehrmacht so they still had electricity when almost everyone else had been cut off.

This then was my happy haven. The bakery was run by three spinsters ladies with hearts of gold. When the loaves of bread came out of the oven, one of the sisters named Hanna would cut off a few good-sized slices, put some butter and sugar on it and give it to me. I couldn't wish for anything more heavenly.

Had I not been so shy, I would have given Hanna a hug that would have made her blush. Every once in a while she would give me a few slices of bread to take home. "Here, for your sick Dad; stick it under your coat so you won't get caught".

When the time came that electricity was no longer available to us, our oldest brother Peter had the answer. He managed to get his hands on a few car or truck batteries, fix them up as well as possible, and put them on a charge. We had two or three of these batteries, and they all had names.

And how did we charge up those batteries when we had no electricity? My older brothers rigged up the rear section of an old bicycle and mounted it in the shed with the rear wheel, without tire, off the floor. A drive belt running from the wheel was connected to a generator. Peter mounted a voltage meter on top, so we could see how the generator would charge once the battery was hooked up to it. On the handlebars was a small reading disk with a little reading light above it, powered by the same generator. All the Zaat children had to take turns peddling the bike to charge up batteries. A list in the kitchen told us whose turn it was next.

Once fully charged, the battery was taken into the house and hooked up to a wooden triangle with three little four-volt light bulbs on it that hung above the table. This provided enough light for one family member to read aloud from a book, while the rest of the family enjoyed the story. When it came time for a change in readers, the next person came close to the limited light source and continued reading. This way we enjoyed precious closeness of parents, brothers and sisters, making the best of difficult circumstances.

It wasn't always books and reading. Music became

a very important part of our lives, singing when the whole family was together. We tried to sing in harmony under the guidance of our older brother Nico. He was the musician in our family since he had recently finished his musical training at the Utrecht School of Church Music. It must have been shortly before the war that Dad bought us a secondhand piano. This would have been a big purchase during the Depression years, on Dad's modest income. But he got his money's worth. Of the nine children, I think five of us took piano lessons from Nico. Gerry and I, along with Nico, chose music as a profession, all with piano as our main instrument.

it was during the winter of that last war year that Nico composed a mass for three-part male choir. Since it was written during the dark, cold winter of 1944-45, the composition was titled In tenebris facta sunt, meaning, In the dark I was created. When Nico was married in August 1946, the family members, along with a few friends, sang the mass in church while a classmate of Nico's directed the 'Zaat choir'. As you can see, it was not all doom and gloom during the war. There was a very close bond amongst fellow citizens.

I leave the curtains open at night

Henny Merkley

Young people in the village went into hiding. Some would be caught at night and thrown in the back of trucks to be taken to Germany. They took our radios - a bad thing for a teenager. People from the cities came begging for food. As we lived in the country and had a garden, chickens, and even a clandestine pig, we were not hungry. My father worked with a threshing machine and brought home grain every night. We put it in the coffee grinder, and with oil that someone pressed out of rapeseed we made pancakes. They stayed with you: very heavy.

We fed many people. They offered us fine linens, silver and gold rings and other things, just for food. Some farmers took all they could get; we did not. We gave what we could give, and that was it. After five years, and so many things that happened, we almost lost our hope.

My sister and I, eighteen and thirteen, had to pick up potatoes for farmers. The potatoes went to the Germans. Often we stopped as the planes came over, shooting at the nearby airport. There were deep holes by the side of the road to jump in, cold and wet.

I hated blackout curtains. To this day I leave the curtains open at night.

The Putten tragedy

Gerrit Top

My family lived in Gelderland on a small farm only eight kilometers from the town of Putten. As winter came, the food shortage in Amsterdam, Rotterdam and The Hague became so severe that the highway was full of people traveling east looking for food. They had to go further and further afield. People were on the road for days, and sometimes we had as many as twenty people sleeping in our loft. Mother gave each a plate of rye porridge in the morning so that they could continue on their way. It was a parade of bicycles, carts and other contraptions on the highway. My older brother and I, together with a man hiding with us, walked thirty kilometers to Apeldoorn pulling a small wagon loaded with food for his family. It was tough, but satisfying to help a family of five without any income.

October 1, 1944 became the saddest day in history for our town and area. On the previous night, the Resistance, (with the help of an Englishman who had gone into hiding after getting stuck on the wrong side of the front after operation Market Garden) had decided to attack a car carrying German officers. One German was killed, another heavily wounded.

It so happened that German troops from the Herman Goering division were present within twenty kilometers. They were instructed that Sunday morning to go from house to house in the town and surrounding area to gather everybody and take them to the school and

87

church. A few people who tried to run away were shot, and a group of men, selected by German collaborators, were put against a wall and told that if anything happened they would be shot first. From the balcony of the church a German officer announced that anybody who had any knowledge of the attack on the Germans should come forward and would be set free. Some who had only heard the shooting were set free, in fact.

The Resistance men involved, mostly around twenty years old, and the Englishman, were probably not in the area any more, or did not hear the announcement. Nobody showed up at any rate. The German officer then announced that all men between eighteen and fifty years old would be taken hostage. My Dad was fifty-one at the time and my oldest brother seventeen. Both had been caught on their way home from church that morning. They were set free after showing their I.D. Those in the 18 to 50 age bracket went first to a local concentration camp, and after about ten days were shipped to Neuengamme Concentration Camp near Hamburg in Germany. It was a train trip of three days in cattle cars, moving only at night for fear of being spotted by planes.

Of the more than six hundred men who had been rounded up in the town of Putten, only forty-eight returned after Liberation. Five of them died afterwards as a consequence of their concentration camp experiences. I lost an uncle and a cousin in the work camps. The mourning of widows and parents was great. One old couple lost six sons, two sons-in-law, and two grandsons. Many lost three or four sons. Many of our neighbours never returned.

During the last days of the war there was still local German resistance, which had to be cleaned up by incoming Canadian forces. A seventy-six-year-old neighbour lost one of his ten milk cows and his horse, struck by shrapnel. He had lost his only son during the roundup the previous fall. In his devastation he said, "Cow dead, horse dead, boy dead, everything dead."

It has to be recorded that not all the German soldiers involved in the roundup of men in October had followed orders. An uncle and neighbour of ours were told to go into hiding, and there may have been more.

During the last days of the war we had German officers move into the farm. They had found the wine cellar at a nearby castle and made good use of it during the day. I can still picture a sixteen-year-old Hitler Youth coming in to salute one of the officers. The officer shook his head and said, "Do we have to win the war with these kids?"

Patriotic colours

Bouk Jobsis

One day my mother was crying because she could not put a meal together. My father hit the table with his fist, and decided he would take care of us any way he could. It was every man for himself then, like the Wild West. No government to obey and we were going to survive and feed ourselves. The Germans had counted all the livestock but in a waterlogged province like Friesland it was not so difficult to keep some animals hidden in outlying areas. There was no energy to pump the land dry, and a lot of land was inundated. It was marvelous when we could skate endlessly in winter, but it was very cold on that flat, windy land.

There was no coal either. My father dug peat near the lakes, dried it, rented a barge and poled it homewards. Then, from the canal he brought the peat home by carrier bicycle. We made do with whatever we had, old clothes and curtains were useful as fabrics. Shoes for growing feet were an insurmountable problem. Wooden shoes, often in patriotic colours, made a comeback. It was a full-time occupation to stay warm, safe, and fed. I still get open sores on my legs sometimes, probably from vitamin deficiency. We dreamed of food, cakes, chocolates, bananas and oranges. I realize we were lucky to live in an agricultural province.

When the British and American planes flew over on their way to Germany it was a reassuring sound that promised us the war would end eventually.

The dykes
had been blown up

Amy Verhagen

I n the last months of the war, as a thirteen-year-old girl from Amsterdam, I stayed on a farm near the small town of Hauwert, in the top of North Holland. My seven-year-old sister had already been sent there, along with many other children.

At first I was on a big dairy farm where I could watch them make cheese and other products. I had never slept in a bedstee before, a bed built into a wall. The food was so amazing, brown bread with butter on it. Even in Hauwert there was a central kitchen where people could get a meal, but this farm family didn't need to go there for food.

I remember that one time the farmer took me to a dentist to have a tooth pulled. It hurt, as there was no freezing. Across the road from us there was a farm with greenhouses. They too had a city girl staying with them. One night, the school principal came over and told the farmer that he had to take in a couple from Den Helder who were being evacuated, so I had to leave. A neighbour's daughter found me another place to live, near the same town. That time I was taken to people on a small apple farm, and stayed there until after Liberation.

We were suddenly notified that the dykes that kept the Wieringermeer polder dry had been blown up. The farmer with whom I stayed wanted to know more, so we took our bikes and went to check it out. It was shocking. It was unbelievable that this had happened. It was deliberate. What we then saw was terribly sad. Houses were under water up to the roof. All kinds of stuff was floating around, furniture, even a small cradle. Where were all the people? The funny thing is that we never saw a German soldier or army truck, like we did in the city. It was very peaceful looking. Back on the farm we went to work, making space in the attic in case we should be flooded out too. It's a long time ago, but I have never forgotten.

We heard about Liberation in May when a couple of fishermen from Volendam came to the door to sell their smoked eels. It was a miracle!

We hid in the doorways

Yvonne Harvey-Shea

n 1943, when I was five years old, I went to live with my Aunt Gré and Uncle Henk for one year. They lived in Hoorn, where there was still enough food because of all the farms. One time we went to visit Mom and Dad in Haarlem, and on the way back to Hoorn the train was bombed. This was just past Enkhuizen. Everyone had to get out quickly. It was one of those little old trains with just one passenger car, one door to the left and one to the right. On the side where we had to jump out there was a big well. A gentleman who had been sitting in the train with us jumped out and then I had to jump. He caught me, and then my aunt came. The man lay right on top of me along the side of the railroad track until the planes were gone. That's something a person never forgets.

I also remember that a few days before the end of the war Dad bought a small, moldy loaf of bread. I believe he paid 200 guilders for it. When we heard that the Germans were finally going to leave the country, my mother, the lady next door and I went to the city, because people were already celebrating. Tanks full of Germans were rolling through the streets, and some sixteen-year-old boys threw little fireworks under the tanks. This scared the soldiers and as we tried to cross the street the soldiers suddenly began to shoot. A young couple was walking past us, and the man was shot. He fell right across my feet, dead. We all ran into a side street to hide in doorways.

The war was very hard on children

Greta Stephany

My maiden name is Greta Aarsen. I was born in Holland, and we lived in a small town, named Wolfheze, surrounded by woods and open fields, and located approximately ten miles from Arnhem.

Our family consisted of twelve people: my parents, grandparents, seven children, and a Jewish boy of seventeen, whom we called Carel. Since my father was in the Resistance, we were hiding people to keep them from getting killed or taken by the Germans. My father worked at the psychiatric hospital in our town, as did most of the people who lived there. There was no other employment.

The war was very hard on children, to say the least. It made an impression on our lives, some negative and some positive. We became mentally stronger than most and can endure more than others. Even though those bad days are far away now, and we live our lives without thinking much about it, there is always that overwhelming emotion when we come in contact with that part of our past. The crying comes from deep within and does not stop, nor can it be controlled until we remove ourselves physically and mentally from that memory or situation. But then it's gone again as fast as it appeared, like a flash or bad dream, and we go on where we left off.

Yes, we were a bunch of pretty messed up kids, and every time I go back to Holland I find people, including my schoolmates, who identify with everything I feel and write about, and that has been a comfort and even a reason to go back and visit, time and again.

I remember the war in flashes, episodes that seem disconnected from each other.

Contributors

Gerry Bijwaard was eight years old, and had a two-year-old brother, when the war broke out. The family lived in Woerden. He and his wife, Patricia, now live in Virginia.

Els Bauman was born in Deventer, but moved to Friesland after her house was bombed. They lived in Franeker until emigrating to Oregon as a family with four children, the youngest one just a baby. Els worked for Montgomery Ward until she started her family. She and her husband have four children, including twins, and four grandchildren, also including twins. They live in Portland, Oregon.

Tony Stroeve escaped from occupied Holland to England in 1943, and was trained to be an RAF pilot. He survived aerial battles as a Spitfire pilot and after Liberation learned to fly bombers in The Netherlands.

Elsa Abma lives in Forest Grove, Oregon.

Petra Poutsma sent in her war story from Tijeras, New Mexico, USA.

Olga Chesbrough was born in 1938 in Den Dolder, near Bilthoven. Her family moved around a lot during the war since her father was active in the Resistance. After the war her parents went to the Dutch East Indies while Olga completed her studies, including time in Switzerland and England. When President Sukarno of newly independent Indonesia expelled all Dutch citizens, the family moved to Canada. Olga moved to the USA when she was twenty-three, married a serviceman in Hawaii, moved around some more, and now lives in Venice, Florida.

Wilhelmus (Bill) Bongers was born in 1933 and lived in Hoorn, North Holland. He later moved to Canada and was active in the Royal Canadian Legion in Bathurst, New Brunswick. His war memories were recorded by the Comité - Hoorn in Dutch, and for the Legion in English. Bill died in 2011 shortly after sending in his contribution for The Dutch In Wartime.

Tina Hofman was born in Zaandam and was four years old shortly before the end of the war. She came to Canada at age 21.

Michael Vanderboon, grew up in The Hague. He now lives in Hidden Valley Lake, CA

Tine Steen-Dekker lived through the war in Enkhuizen, North Holland. She makes her home in Edmonton, Alberta.

John In 't Hout was nine years old and lived in Scheveningen at the beginning of the war. John sold his shop to one son in 1984, and with his wife moved to the USA where another son already lived. By now the In 't Houts have eight great-grandchildren. John lives in Caledonia, Michigan.

Pauline Hofman was born in Amsterdam, but her family moved away from the city to be near relatives in a more rural area. She now lives in Geneva, Nevada.

Nan Casey was seventeen years old and worked for the Dutch national telephone company when the Germans invaded. She lived in Zeist near Utrecht, where she stayed for the duration of the war. Two days after Liberation in May of 1945 she met a Canadian soldier, Frank 'Red' Casey. In July they were engaged, but they had to wait until December before they were allowed to marry. Frank returned to Canada in January of 1946 and Nan followed him in September on a ship full of war brides from all over Europe. They settled in Penticton, British Columbia, where Frank worked in the Nickel Plate gold mine. After seven years they moved to Saskatoon, where Nan still lives.

Lisette de Groot was born in the Dutch East Indies. When she was three years old her mother died and she went to stay with an aunt and uncle in Rotterdam for two and a half years. Her father remarried, and the family was living in Voorschoten when the war broke out. Lisette and her husband emigrated to Jacksonville, Florida in 1964 to work at the American office of a Dutch company. They retired to Asheville, North Carolina, where they still live.

Rita Binder grew up in Stadskanaal in the province of Groningen, but when she was fourteen years old her family moved to Gouda before the war. This is where she lived during the war. In the late 1940s she came to Canada on her own and met her husband there. Rita has five children and six grandchildren, and lives in Wahnapitae, near Sudbury, Ontario.

Martha Gubbels lived in Brabant and was eight when the war broke out. In 1955 her family emigrated to Canada. She and her first husband, Jan van de Ven, had six children. After his death, she remarried but was widowed again.

Martha now lives in Strathroy, Ontario. The Catholic church in Strathroy, at one time had 40% Dutch members and 40% Portuguese, which means there are lots of Dutch immigrants to socialize with.

Adriana Lyffyt was born in Rotterdam in 1941. She now lives in Gilroy, California.

Minie Kerstholt came to Canada on the Sibajak in 1952 with husband and son. She sent in her war memories from Kingston, Ontario.

Jacoba J. Bessey lived in Haarlem when the war began, one of four girls. Her brother Hans was born in 1941. She now lives in Regina, Saskatchewan.

Nelia Barnfield was two years old at the beginning of the war. Her family lived in Enschede, but moved to Leiden in 1941. She now lives in Victoria, British Columbia.

John Keulen was born near Chicago in 1931 to Dutch immigrant parents. The family returned to The Netherlands when John was two years old and settled in the Frisian village of Bakhuizen. John's parents emigrated to the United States for a second time, in 1948, accompanied by John, then seventeen, and his brother. John lives in Port Orange, Florida.

Johanna Opdam and her family lived in Lisse, a place in South Holland that is famous for its flower bulbs. She now lives in Grimsby, Ontario.

Frank VanderKley lived with his family in The Hague. He was six when the war began. He emigrated to Canada in 1953 to escape the military draft and found work on a farm in Alberta. He later became a lawyer.

Enno Reckendorf was ten years old when the war started. He now makes his home in Hertford, North Carolina.

Harm Duursma was born in Groningen in 1915. He moved to Hengelo in 1937, where he worked at the Dickers foundry. He was the father of two infant children when the war broke out and was called up to report to Rotterdam for military service. He returned to work at the Dickers plant in 1941. He and his family emigrated to Canada in 1953. He contributed his war memories at age 95, living in White Rock, British Columbia.

Henry van Ommen was born in 1932, and was almost eight years old when the war began. He came to Canada in 1953 and died in 2010.

Richard Oostra grew up in Leeuwarden, Friesland. He was six when the war broke out. He came to Canada in 1951 at age seventeen, got work and bought a car within the first year. He got busy socializing with Canadian girls and worked hard at becoming a Canadian. Then, after nine years, he married a woman who was the opposite of what he had been looking for: She was Dutch and blond. They had four children.

John Looyenga was born in the Frisian town of Bozum in 1934. During the war he was old enough to help his father with the work of moving freight to Leeuwarden, the province's capital. John emigrated to Canada with his parents and three siblings in 1951 and now lives on the edge of Acton, Ontario.

Marijke Shaban was born in Delft in 1941. Her family, with three brothers at the time, moved to Canada in 1951, where another brother was born. Her father died in 1958. Her mother then married a Canadian war veteran who lived on Manitoulin Island, Ontario.

Anne Hendren was twelve years old at the start of the war, living in Utrecht. She now lives in Salem, Oregon.

Cornelius (Con) Zaat grew up in the village of Kwintsheul, in the province of South Holland. During the early 1950s the Canadian forces were advertising in Dutch music magazines for musicians to help build up military bands across the country. Con's brother signed up first, and Con followed a year later, coming to Prince Edward Island in 1955. He played clarinet, bassoon, saxophone, as well as several other instruments. He later taught music in the schools and played in the Island's symphony orchestra in his spare time. Con's civic marriage had taken place before he left Holland, but his wife was not able to come to Canada until five months later, when the marriage was blessed in the church. Con continues to live in Montague, Prince Edward Island.

Henny Merkley contributed her war memories from Thunder Bay, Ontario.

Gerrit Top grew up near Putten in Gelderland. He now lives in High River, Alberta.

Bouk Jobsis worked as a midwife in The Netherlands before coming to the United States in 1964, having delivered more than two hundred babies. She has also lived in Iran. She settled in Houston, Texas, after a year in Utah. Bouk has two daughters.

Amy Verhagen was born in Amsterdam. She was sent to a North Holland farm during the war because of severe food shortages in the major cities. She moved to Toronto, Ontario in 1954, and now she and her husband make their home in Dartmouth, Nova Scotia.

Yvonne Harvey-Shea lives in Stanwood, Washington.

Greta Stephany lived in Wolfheze, a small town near Arnhem, during the war. She was eleven years old at the time of Operation Market Garden, also known as the Battle of Arnhem. She came to the USA in 1956.

The Dutch in Wartime series

Book 1
Invasion

Edited by:
Tom Bijvoet

90 pages paperback
ISBN: 978-0-9868308-0-8

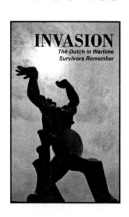

Book 2
Under Nazi Rule

Edited by:
Tom Bijvoet

88 pages paperback
ISBN: 978-0-9868308-3-9

Book 3
Witnessing the Holocaust

Edited by:
Tom Bijvoet

96 pages paperback
ISBN: 978-0-9868308-4-6

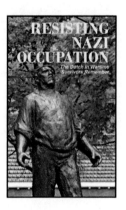